10 POWERFUL NETWORKING TIPS USING SOCIAL MEDIA

START CONVERSATIONS AND ATTRACT QUALITY LIFETIME CONNECTIONS POWER NETWORKING IN A SOCIAL MEDIA WORLD

By

CARL E. REID, CSI

Foreword By
Biba Pedron
The Connection Queen

If you purchase a
PAPERBACK copy of
*10 Powerful Networking
Tips Using Social Media,*
RECEIVE A REWARD

You get to **register FREE** for
Upcoming Interactive Webinar;
*Power Networking In A
Social Media World*
($95 VALUE)
**Learn Networking Secrets not
published in the book** to be a
rainmaker in your network. **After
your purchase** REGISTER at
CarlEReid.com
From menu click on *Books* >
Free Webinar Registration

Other Books by Carl E. Reid

10 Powerful Networking Secrets of Influential People
10 Powerful Networking Tips Using Business Cards – Global Extended Edition

PLEASE WRITE A BOOK REVIEW AT
Amazon.com/author/carlereid

REVIEWS ABOUT THIS BOOK

Communication today is through conversations on social media. Managing these conversations helps one build a strong personal and business brand. Towards that Carl E Reid's book is an excellent guide that gives you all you need to know for each channel to create conversations that deliver you the value with your community. - **Joy Abdullah**, Co-Founder 3MinuteMarketing.biz

"10 Powerful Networking Tips Using Social Media" connects all the dots and demystifies the functionality of each platform in an easy to follow plan that will benefit the novice and savvy business owner in building a powerful and sustainable network. -**Angela M. Spencer**, President & Co-founder Spencer's Angel Works **AngelaMSpencer.com**

Carl E. Reid has done it again. His new book is not only timely but also unique. With the advent of technology that rapidly changes our lives, Carl is ahead of the curve by offering job seekers and everybody else what we need for tomorrow: the effective use of social media tools, which is instrumental by going beyond survival and into prosperity. Carl's detailed and logical explanations make for lively reading with plentiful links to relevant resources. Bravo! - **Alex Freund**, Career and Interview Coach LandingExpert.com

This is Social Media 101! What a great resource! This is a great way to step into the 21st century and learn new ways of connecting to your brand, business, people in so many ways! -**Karen B. Murray** Founder of Running To Health And Happiness

Any way you look at it, other people are your greatest asset. Carl E. Reid's in-depth, easy to follow social media networking guide will fill your career with opportunities to meet people and reap the rewards. - **Rod Colon**, Author, Motivational Speaker and Master Networker **RodColon.com**

"10 Powerful Networking Tips Using Social Media" was a great read!! The explanations led me from beginning to end without skipping anything. Once again, job well done to help all of us in the industry. Thank you Carl!! -**Kim Popek**, Real Estate Professional

"10 Powerful Networking Tips Using Social Media" is an invaluable 21st Century resource. Carl Reid shares years of expert tech leadership and business insight to make navigating the social media landscape a breeze. This book is a must for understanding and optimizing social media both personally and professionally. -**James "Koe" Rodriguez**, Artist & Entrepreneur, **ATWcrew.com**

This is a wonderful resource by Carl E. Reid! Easy to read and understand, no matter what your prior experience is with Social Media. I was lucky enough to read the draft manuscript, thanks to Carl. I highly recommend this book to everyone! -**Christine Dykeman**, Certified Human Resources Professional

ACKNOWLEDGEMENTS

Many thanks to my Editor, **Jacquie Adorno** who provided much attention to detail to make sure readers received useful information that is actionable.

Thanks to my very successful wife and business partner, **Phyllis M. Shelton** for her patience, understanding and encouragement throughout the years. She helped me overcome many challenges.

Special thanks to my business mentors, **Julio** and **Mayra Barreto**, for challenging me to push beyond my limits by empowering other people with 1 on 1 per chance conversations and discussions through social media connections.

This Book Is Dedicated To . . .

My father **Joseph A. Reid**, a man who never knew a stranger. He took me on Indiana Jones like adventures within and outside the United States, while teaching me life values, how to develop a people network through benevolence and public speaking skills.

My mother, **Mercedes V. Reid**, who taught me etiquette, appreciation of various cultures and always reminded me "There is never a good excuse for bad manners".

My siblings, **Laura, Lyle, Bruce** and **Noel** who love and supported me throughout the years, despite my imperfections.

My favorite [only] daughter **Tiana K. Reid** whose journey through life I have witnessed has been just as educational for me as it has been for her with our discussions and travel adventures.

My First Baptist Church, Bronxville NY family who embraces me with their love through lively fellowship discussions and my **Pastor, Rev. Lamont S. Granby** who counsels me every Sunday to be better, care better and forgive better with uplifting people.

All my extended family and people in my off-line and online social media international global network, who have shared a kind word, listened to my ideas or pinged me via email, phone or text message to just say "Hey".

My very dear friend **Edward P. Helck,** whose generous heart, quick wit and zest for life through funny story telling, impacted any person who crossed his path.

Contents

Foreword By Biba Pédron.............................10

Introduction 12

Different Types Of Social Media 16

Social Media Networking Uses 17

Quick Start Social Media Buzz Words 19

Tools To Elevate, Monitor and Protect Your Brand ..23

Prepare To Attract Opportunities 25

Best Days And Times To post 26

1. LINKEDIN Is My Business 28

2. FACEBOOK Is My Friend 36

3. TWITTER Is My Micro Blog 44

4.INSTAGRAM Is My Photo Journal.........49

5.MEETUP Is My Face To Face 57

6. ALIGNABLE Is My Local Community 63

7. BUMBLE BIZZ Is My Quick Connection 70

8. WHATSAPP Is My Group Message Center..........74

9.YOUTUBE Is My Learning Library.........79

10. QUORA Is My Expert...........................84

11. Bonus: Zoom Is My Video Conference Meeting .90

12. Bonus: Cell Phone Is My Communication Hub...93

13. Bonus: Email Is My Integrated Social Center 97

Social Media Security 103

Health And Wellness Work Life Balance 106

Vanity Domain Be Thy Name 109

Social Media Scheduling Tools...............................111

Social Media Glossary Of Terms 113

Global Directory Of Social Media Sites...................130

About The Author..147

Additional Publications By Carl E. Reid 148

FOREWORD BY BIBA PÉDRON

Are you thinking of boosting your business with social media? Start here.

I met Carl E. Reid many years ago when I was organizing networking events in New York. The reason we connected immediately, was because we had the same passion to connect and help people, with tips, network and resources. And even if now that I live between Miami and France, we don't get the chance to meet very often, we are always connected, and he is somebody that I can always count on.

In this book Carl offers a compelling overview of everything you need to use networking and social media effectively to attract more clients. He sets thing out as a step by step guide with no way to get confused, lost or take a wrong turn. He gives you the purpose of every platform, why and how to you them. Then you just need to implement it. EASY

Reading this book, will save you a lot of time and mone and fast track your success. When you know who is your target market, and the business approach you want for your business, Carl tells you which platform to use, to be more effective.

Written by someone who is a successful serial entrepreneur, who knows what the word "connect"

11

really means and always served people to grow their businesses, "10 POWERFUL NETWORKING TIPS USING SOCIAL MEDIA" is a practical, no-nonsense, information-packed bible to boost your business with social media. Carl uses his decades of experience connecting people with one another to help you build value relationships. This easy to use guide will help you navigate your way to also becoming a successful entrepreneur well connected.

I have personally used social media for years in my business to get international clients, but I still learned new information and resources with Carl's book.

Biba Pédron
Business & Mindset Coach
The Connection Queen and Author of 3 best seller books.

In English . . . "Stop Pitching And Start Networking" "Start Your Dream Business Today"

In French . . . "Sauter le Pas"

www.BibaPedron.com
www.Facebook.com/bibapedronfans

INTRODUCTION

Being a professional blogger since 2004 I have watched the social media landscape develop into a world of possibilities for everyone globally. Social media levels the playing field for individual people and all size businesses to spotlight their voice or brand to expand market share opportunities.

Whether you are new to social media or have been a player on the field for some time, this book is written to help bring your networking engagements to the next level to achieve personal, career or business goals.

Since every social media platform has a different culture, this book will serve as a reference guide to help you make people connections using appropriate network etiquette approaches. Depending your goals every platform is not necessarily for everyone . . . meaning you don't to have a presence on all social media.

I selected 10 social media platforms to provide a cross section of different sites proven to work best for high impact networking engagements. Following each chapter title categories follow to help you identify platforms that may work best for your personal goals. A comprehensive list of other social media platforms around the world is also published at the end of this book.

How To Use This Book

The chapters are independent of each other. This book is presented as a reference guide so you can go straight a chapter of interest. For example, if you want information about using Instagram, you only need to read that chapter. This allows you to immediately hang out at each respective social platform, while using the social networking techniques and features you learned from the book.

The table of contents in the digital version of this book allows you to go directly to each chapter.

Rather than being on all sites, I recommend you focus on learning 1 or 2 social media platforms well, like LinkedIn and Twitter. Then move to a new site, spending a decent amount of time practicing the social networking techniques from the book until you feel comfortable making connections.

Lastly, have fun and enjoy the exhilarating ride that social media networking offers for making lifetime associations to produce results for you or your team.

HELP IS A PHONE CALL AWAY

My company SavvyIntrapreneur.com provides social media networking 1-On-1, Group webinars, LIVE video conference training and telephone support options.

DIFFERENT TYPES OF SOCIAL MEDIA

Social networks—Connect with people
Facebook, Twitter, LinkedIn

Media sharing networks
Instagram, Snapchat, YouTube

Discussion forums—Share news and ideas
Reddit, Quora, Digg

Bookmarking and content curation networks
Pinterest, Flipboard

Consumer review networks
Yelp, Zomato, TripAdvisor

Blogging and publishing networks
WordPress, Tumblr, Medium, Twitter, Blogger

Social shopping networks
Polyvore, Etsy, Fancy

Interest-based networks
Goodreads, Houzz, Last.fm

Sharing economy networks
Airbnb, Uber, Taskrabbit

Anonymous social networks
Whisper, Ask.fm, After School

Social Media Networking Uses

Sharing Value Information

With social media, you can share information and ideas in a variety of ways. Different outlets allow you to publish your own ideas in writing, with pictures, or through videos and voice recordings; and you can also hyperlink your audience to interesting articles, images, and videos. The information you share can be either private or public. For example, you can email a private message to one person and broadcast a video to a global audience via YouTube. Always consider your communication situation (see page 68) before sharing information.

Learning New Information

Social media can also serve as personal learning tools. You can get updates about your friends and family or learn about what is happening in your community and around the world. The immediacy of the information flow allows you to get the gist of the latest news almost as it happens. Today, breaking news is often broadcast via social media before traditional media like TV and newspapers cover it in detail. Social media can also reveal public sentiment about the big issues of the day or, on a less urgent level, opinions about a new restaurant or movie.

Interacting

Maybe the most powerful element of social media is their interactive nature. Social media break the traditional barriers of time and distance between people. With video chat technologies like Skype, you can talk to people face-to-face anywhere in the world. On Facebook and mobile devices, you can chat digitally and text with your friends and family. Twitter even allows you to interact with media members, public officials, professional athletes, and celebrities.

Marketing

More and more, social media are being used for marketing purposes. Businesses use social media to promote themselves and their products. Nonprofit organizations raise funds and promote charity events. Individuals market themselves to prospective employers. And you can use social media to promote ideas and events that are important to you.

Let's Have a Conversation

How do you use social media? Which networking uses above do you include in your social media travels? Have you used social media in other ways? I look forward to your response via email iGetSmart@savvyintrepreneur.com.

Quick Start Social Media Buzz Words

1. Engagement

'Engagement' refers to any action taken by a social media user on your page. This can be in the form of 'Likes', 'Reactions', 'Shares' or 'Comments'.

For example, if a user on your Facebook page has 'reacted' to your post by choosing to 'Like' it, they have engaged with that particular post. And those engagements can add up very quickly.

2. Ephemeral content

'Ephemeral' refers to content on social media platforms that disappear after a set period of time. This type of content is seen most frequently on Facebook, Instagram and Snapchat.

For example, Instagram Stories (and Facebook Stories) are limited to a lifespan of 24 hours. On Snapchat, messages to friends disappear as soon as the user has left the app — after having opened the message.

3. Filter

'Filters' are used on certain social media platforms as a way for people to edit their photos. Each filter offers an overlaid effect that can be placed onto images. This feature is most popularly used on Instagram (#NoFilter — not).

4. Handle

A 'handle' refers to a user's account name on Twitter, but it can be in reference to other social platforms, too. Each 'handle' is unique and can be used to find or mention other people on the platform.

A user's handle is the '@' symbol, followed by their account name.

5. Hashtag

A 'hashtag' on social media refers to any word or phrase that is following the '#', or hashtag, symbol.

Hashtags are used on social media as a way to find content about a specific topic, or as a way to make a user's content more discoverable to other people.

For example, if a user posted on social media using '#futureoftech', they could find other people' content about that topic by clicking on the hashtag.

On Twitter, popular topics, or hashtags, can be found in the 'Trending Topics' section of the page.

6. Lens

Not to be confused with a 'Filter', a 'Lens' is an animated overlay effect that is used while people are taking a photo of themselves, also known as a 'selfie'. The lens can animate the user's image while in camera mode to appear as anything — from a dog sticking its tongue out to a cat with glasses (yes, we're serious).

7. Impression

'Impressions' are the number of times on social media have seen your posts. For example, if five people have seen your post on Facebook, that means you have five impressions for that post.

The maximum number of 'impressions' your post can have is the number of people you are connected to on Facebook — but remember, if someone else shares your post, you can gain impressions from all of their Facebook friends too.

8. Share

'Shares' refer to the number of times any user's piece of content has been re-posted on social media. The 'Share' feature on social media is a clickable button that allows you to repost content other people post to your own timeline (that's your own personal newsfeed).

For example, if a user clicks on the 'Share' button on Facebook, they'll have the option of sharing that post either with another friend, on their News Feed or via Facebook Messenger.

9. Story

A 'Story' — either on Instagram or on Facebook — is a collection of photos or videos compiled into one album that can be shared with other people on the platform.

These Stories disappear after 24 hours, making them ephemeral.

Tools To Elevate, Monitor and Protect Your Brand

"It takes 20 years to build a reputation and five minutes to ruin it." -Warren Buffet

Who's Talking About You or Your Company?

As a result of criteria you type into Google Alerts Google.com/alerts it will send you an email as soon as any related Internet postings based your key words, topics or even your name.

If you're a student writing a paper or need recent references for a report, Google Alerts is great for automating your research.

Google Alerts is a great tool to know immediately know who and what people are saying about you or your company. This positions you to get in front of it and resolve issues before they impact your reputation.

VIDEO: How To Setup Google Alerts
Tinyurl.com/HowToUseGoogleAlerts
By TheHelpfuldad YouTube Channel

Acquire Current Email and Telephone Numbers for LinkedIn Connections

SignalHire.com works within LinkedIn's terms of service (TOS). Since LinkedIn no longer publishes email addresses for your network connections, SignalHire is an excellent tool for finding an email address and phone number for your contacts.

SignalHire finds and verifies emails across the Internet in real-time. This keeps LinkedIn contact emails and telephone numbers up to date. You can also extract personal and business emails for LinkedIn connections.

ADDITIONAL MONITORING RESOURCES

Brand24.com

BrandYourself.com

YouScan.io

Reputation.com

BrandMentions.com

GatherUp.com

Buzzsumo.com

Reputology.com

Mention.com

ReviewPush.com

SimilarWeb.com

Your Web Browser – Google your full name regularly

The Brand Grader onlinereputation.io/brand-grader

Social searcher social-searcher.com/social-mention

25

PREPARE TO ATTRACT OPPORTUNITIES

"Success occurs when opportunity meets preparation"
-Zig Ziglar

Various components add to creating a social media profile that maintains a consistent brand across All social media.

Take a professional photo or have someone take a picture of you just head and shoulders. No selfies. Photos create trust. No photo, No trust.

Create a succinct brand sentence of 160 to 200 characters that describes your skills and interests.

Create a cover page used on sites like LinkedIn, Twitter, Facebook

Invest in a branded vanity domain YourFirstLastName.com that reflects your name. If your name domain is taken, add your middle initial or generational identifier (i.e. Jr, Sr, III etc.) that makes your brand unique.

Best Days And Times To post

"What you post online speaks VOLUME about who you really are. POST with intention. REPOST with caution." – Germany Kent

According to a recent article by SproutSocial.com below are the best days and times to post by social media platform. Keep in mind these times may vary in the future due to a huge number of people working from home in 2020. Work hours and mindset are different working from home vs. working in an office building. Days and times can also vary by industry.

Best times to post on LinkedIn

Best times: Wednesday from 8–10AM and 12 noon, Thursday at 9 AM and 1–2PM and Friday at 9AM
Worst day: Sunday

Best times to post on Twitter

Best times: Wednesday and Friday at 9AM
Worst day: Saturday

BEST TIMES TO POST ON FACEBOOK

Best times: Wednesday, 11AM and 1–2PM
Worst day: Sunday

BEST TIMES TO POST ON INSTAGRAM

Best times: Wednesday at 11AM and Friday from
10AM – 11AM
Worst day: Sunday

1. LINKEDIN IS MY BUSINESS

BUSINESS | CAREER |PROFESSIONAL NETWORKING | GROUPS | BLOGGING

"The fastest way to change yourself is to hang out with people who are already the way you want to be."
Reid Hoffman, LinkedIn founding partner

1. DESCRIPTION

LinkedIn.com is the only social media platform that nearly emulates professional business networking, which is THE most effective process to achieve success in any endeavor in the 21st century than it ever was in the 20th century. LinkedIn focuses on empowering professionals who are very serious about developing mutually beneficial business relationships. It enables you to network and build your professional portfolio. Still, you can also go out into the world and look for a new job. ... It is also a sourcing tool used by employers and recruiters who are looking for job candidates.

2. LINKEDIN NETWORKING BENEFITS

1. Establish a professional brand identity that attracts career and business opportunities
2. International Global reach to connect with "like-minded" business professionals.

3. Knowledge exchange.
4. Opportunity to become a social media influencer and develop relationships with other influencers.
5. Publishing LinkedIn articles helps establish you as a subject matter expert.
6. Gain exposure to Hiring Managers, Recruiters, and Talent Directors.
7. Demonstrate your knowledge, credibility, and leadership expertise.
8. LinkedIn is a remarkable research tool.
9. You can gain social proof for your skills and talents.
10. Follow Companies and People for "in the Know" business intelligence.
11. LinkedIn Groups allow staying on top of the market and industry trends.

3. LINKEDIN POWER NETWORKING TIPS

Below are six tips to help you to engage people and start conversations with people in your network.

1. START TALKING TO BE A HIGHLY VISIBLE INFLUENCER

There are three actions that separate spectators (lurkers) from social media influencers. Your "Engagement Mindset" either stymies or expands your sphere of influence by sending hidden messages to your network. Understand the hidden message you send to your system with your LIKE, COMMENT, and SHARE actions to LinkedIn posts.

LIKE = That's nice, but I couldn't care less. If you act invisible, you will be hidden. In other words, wasting time LIKING a post sends the message, "I'm OK with settling for being invisible. Since a LIKE is THE least effective way for people to notice you, a LIKE result is...

- There can be no complaints that no one notices or acknowledges you.
- You don't receive LinkedIn invitations to connect and
- No LinkedIn Inbox messages that start conversations to explore mutually beneficial interests or opportunities.

COMMENT = Contribute to starting or contributing to the conversation with your thoughts, views, or appreciation for the value of information shared in a post.

SHARE = THE ultimate power networking edification action. You send the message I value your information so much, I want to add value to my network by sharing your post to benefit my community. This makes you the center of your network.

THE POWER OF SHARING

With 150+ shares this post started a conversation with almost 500,000 views and new connections added.

Carl E. Reid, CSI, ECC
Speaker/Author, CEO @intersections of Tech, Leadership, Business Mentorship, ...
10mo • 🌐

This is brilliant for identifying #talent that fits into #corporate #culture!!
_____
#business #innovation #innovation #leadership

Barbara Corcoran Swears by 1 Interview Question to Weed Out Complainers
inc.com

😊😍👏 699 • 86 Comments

Reactions

👍 Like   💬 Comment   ↪ Share   Most Relevant ▾

📈 497,645 views of your post in the feed

Barbara Corcoran Swears by 1 Interview Question to Weed Out Complainers   411 reactions 47 comments

1,093 people from Accenture viewed your post	18,133 people who have the title Salesperson viewed your post	10,749 people viewed your post from Bengaluru Area, India
EY — 956		Greater New York City Area — 9,885
IBM — 863	Software Developer — 15,234	London, United Kingdom — 7,720
Tata Consultancy Services — 852	Project Manager — 7,387	New Delhi Area, India — 6,983
Cognizant — 694	Engineer — 7,222	Mumbai Area, India — 6,814
Capgemini — 580	Student — 7,160	Paris Area, France — 5,203
Infosys — 554	Information Technology Consultant — 6,860	São Paulo Area, Brazil — 4,147
Microsoft — 550	Consultant — 6,802	Kalyan Area, India — 3,692
Oracle — 476	Executive Director — 6,729	Hyderabad Area, India — 3,447

33

2. GIVE AND RECEIVE RECOMMENDATIONS AND ENDORSEMENTS

The best way to receive LinkedIn recommendations is by writing a recommendation for people in your LinkedIn network.

Write recommendations to assemble a sales team to attract raving evangelists that talk up your brand. Learn how to engage a silent sales team by reading my article "Have You Used LinkedIn's No Cost Sales Team Tool To Attract Clients Or Job Opportunities?" https://tinyurl.com/CEReidLinkedInRecommendations

3. BECOME THE CENTER OF YOUR NETWORK BY STARTING A GROUP

4. Power networkers avoid using LinkedIn "Canned" messages as they are incredibly impersonal. Write personal notes for

- LinkedIn connection invitations
- Birthday wishes
- New Job congratulations
- Job anniversary wishes

5. JOIN GROUPS

6. START A GROUP

LINKEDIN NETWORKING EXERCISE

Explain the difference between sending a connection invite Vs. only Following a person.

ADDITIONAL LINKEDIN RESOURCES

Excellent article by Maria Raybould with an awesome Infographic "What Will Make You Stand Out on LinkedIn in 2020: The Expert Insights You Need to See."
https://tinyurl.com/LinkedInStandOut2020

Hubspot.com has an excellent PDF resource document "*Learn LinkedIn From The Experts.*"
https://tinyurl.com/LearnLinkedInFromTheExperts

Free PDF document download of "*How To Really Use LinkedIn*" is an excellent book by Jan Vermeiren and Bert Verndonck
https://tinyurl.com/HowToReallyUseLinkedinBook
Note: This document may contain links that no longer work, but it is still an excellent Linkedin beginner reference resource.

Articles By Carl E. Reid
10 Powerful Linkedin Networking Tips (Part I)
https://tinyurl.com/CEReidLinkedInNetworkingPartI

10 Powerful Linkedin Networking Tips (PART II)
https://tinyurl.com/CEReidLinkedInNetworkingPartII

LET'S HAVE A CONVERSATION

Please send me a LinkedIn invitation to connect or follow me at LinkedIn.com/in/CarlEReid

2. FACEBOOK Is My Friend

"Some people need to realize Facebook is a social network, not a diary" -Unknown

SOCIALIZE | PHOTO SHARING | BUSINESS PAGES | GROUPS | CAUSES

Facebook.com is the largest social networking site on planet Earth and one of the most widely used. Facebook was perhaps the first that surpassed the landmark of 1 billion user accounts. It has become a perfect platform for B2C (business to consumer) marketing, providing very targeted advertising opportunities based on user's likes and associations. What about connections with friends and family? It allows you to share holiday pictures and video clips from your android and iPhone with your social circle. Even your old browsing Nokia is not left out.

NETWORKING BENEFITS

1. To maintain a good relationship with others who identify with particular tastes or products.
2. Announce essential things regarding your products/services.
3. Create brands for individuals and businesses.
4. Create a personal portfolio (Profile branding).
5. Ask public opinion, ask questions.
6. Communicate and collaborate with people across distance.

7. It allows for an open communication channel. That is, customers can ask questions they may be uncomfortable asking in person or on the phone.
8. It's significant for people seeking massive recognition.
9. With its enormous user base, Facebook gives marketers a close limitless audience for commercial messages/ brand awareness.
10. It allows business people to target message delivery using a piece of varying demographic information like location age, relationship status, and even sexual preference.
11. It also provides an array of analytical tools that marketers can use to gauge advertising effectiveness and adjust ads as necessary.
12. Facebook allows organizations/employers to know more about their prospective employees before approving the employee's application.
13. Facebook allows people to reconnect with long time family and friends. Facebook enables people to share their opinions about a subject matter.
14. It can be used to coarse or influence people's thoughts or choices about a product or services. This also includes decisions about the personality of a person either for or against.
15. Using Facebook ads allows business owners to boost their website traffic.

FACEBOOK POWER NETWORKING TIPS

SHOW YOUR PERSONALITY

Your favorite subjects for Facebook status updates reveal more about your personality than may intend, according to psychologists. From posting a photo of yourself with your partner to sharing your daily gym exercise routine, status topics have been found to be linked to key personality traits. This could either mar or allow you to tie quality relationships that could affect the user positively. One of the things that could defend you in the face of intense competition for jobs, grant opportunities, scholarships, and other relevant opportunities is your perceived trait from the viewpoint of employers or helpers. Post like pictures, videos, and words matter a lot.

CREATE A GROUP

Facebook group is a space for like-minded people with similar interests to connect. Allowing your audience to establish and grow new relationships within your group will reflect on your company as a place they can trust and respect. It will enable your audience to have full insight into the goal of the group or on product and services offerings.

It also helps to build lasting relationships with your audience. Your audience or customers give room for product and services improvement through complaints and suggestions. It also helps to test a product idea before sharing it with the public. The feedback of your audience enables you to make wise decisions/ improvement of your product and services. The group also serves as an online community for your audience to network.

JOIN A FACEBOOK GROUP

Benefits of Facebook Groups for Business

- Build a better relationship.
- A free platform to promote your activities and business daily.
- It allows you to download relevant information helpful in your niche.
- It helps you to meet and network with new members within your space.
- It allows fellow people to keep track of your product and services.

CREATE AN AD

Social media is a great way to increase exposure and traffic for your business, create devoted customers, and generate leads and sales.

Facebook remains a leading Social Network. It is the go-to social platform for the many marketers and for a good reason. If you aren't already advertising on Facebook, you should be advertising on Facebook, especially if you want to grow to a high degree. And to build your brand and create new demand for your products and services.

NINE REASONS FACEBOOK ADS WILL HELP YOUR BUSINESS BRAND GROW

People Spend an unbelievable amount of time on social media.

The average American spends about 40 minutes on Facebook- Liking and sharing content. More than 4.1 million posts, status updates, and photos every minute.

Facebook has a large, active userbase that spends an unbelievable amount of time every day of every month.

REACH OUT, CONNECT, NETWORK

If you want customers or audiences to discover your business, you need to use Facebook ads services. The best part of the story is you don't need a huge budget. A little token will put you or your message in front of 5000 to 100000 people. You also have the option of choosing your target audience in terms of age, geographical location, and lifestyle.

ENHANCED TARGETING

People can potentially be targeted with Facebook ads based on their location, demographics, age, gender, interest, behavior, and connections.

REMARKETING/ RETARGETING

Facebook retargeting is the process of finding people who've visited your website and then using their information to find their Facebook profiles.

Retargeting is a form of advertising that brings back website visitors.

FACEBOOK ENGAGEMENT TOOLS

One major thing that encourages user's experience on Facebook is getting feedbacks on your post either through likes, emojis, and comments.

Here are the ways to engage your audience:

- Post every time
- Put pictures in your comments
- Like and reply to other people's post
- Boost your posts using Facebook ads

ADDITIONAL FACEBOOK RESOURCES

Educational article by PCMAG "*22 Hidden Facebook Features Only Power Users Know*"
https://www.pcmag.com/news/22-hidden-facebook-features-only-power-users-know

"How to Use Facebook: A Beginner's Guide" By Clifford Chi Follow on Twitter: @BigRedDawg16
https://blog.hubspot.com/marketing/how-to-use-facebook

10 (Almost) Effortless Ways to Boost Facebook Engagement by Pat Parkinson https://www.postplanner.com/boost-facebook-engagement-infographic/

Security Features and Tips by Facebookhttps://www.facebook.com/help/285695718429403

How to Use Facebook Groups for Networking & Job Searchhttps://www.thebalancecareers.com/how-to-use-facebook-groups-for-networking-and-job-search-4589758

How to create a group on Facebook

https://www.postplanner.com/how-to-create-a-facebook-group/

https://www.dummies.com/social-media/facebook/how-to-create-a-facebook-group/

How to create a Facebook account

https://web.facebook.com/help/188157731232424?helpref=topq&_rdc=1&_rdr

What are the advantages of using Facebook?

https://www.quora.com/What-are-the-advantages-of-using-Facebook

 How to use Facebook ads

Let's Have A Conversation

Mosey over to my Facebook business page Facebook.com/CarlEReid and give it a LIKE

3. TWITTER IS MY MICRO BLOG
MICRO BLOGGING | NEWS | BUSINESS

"Think twice before you speak, because your words and influence will plant the seed of either success or failure in the mind of another." -Napoleon Hill

Twitter.com social networking site enables you to post short text messages (called tweets), containing a limited number of characters (up to 280), to convey your message to the world. With the growing craze for online shopping, Twitter also makes it possible to promote your businesses and even shop directly through tweets. Twitter doesn't allow you to share your life story. It is built with a sense of intelligence that makes people act smart and develop a good understanding of summary.

Imagine that you have an opportunity to meet the richest person on earth, and you have just sixty seconds to speak and convince him of your business idea. What will you say? Keep in mind that a missed opportunity might take another decade to access.

Twitter puts you in that position every time. You use your tweets to convince your audience to see what you are driving at. Your ability to be succinct is tested with each tweet. How will you respond by writing less to convince your audience?

TWITTER NETWORKING BENEFITS

1. Reach a large number of people quickly through tweets and retweets.
2. Build relationships with experts and other followers.
3. Get on-the-spot feedback about your products and services.
4. Promote your blog content—videos, Presentations, etc.
5. Get traffic to your website.
6. Keep up with the latest trends in your industry. Follow up people and organizations in your line of interest.
7. It helps to find out what people are saying about you.
8. It makes you more informed
9. It unleashes your killer instinct.
10. Become the talk of your community
11. Facebook Offers you a unique opportunity to the wisdom of great men within your circle.
12. Its' originality is 100% such that your tweets define your personality, and your words are duly followed. For example, Any official account talks about real-time news or the real personality of the user.

TWITTER POWER NETWORKING BENEFITS

BUILD AN ATTRACTIVE AND QUALITY PROFILE

- Have a profile picture and cover image of the company, often accounts without photos do not inspire confidence.
- Use relevant hashtags in your description to increase your traffic, visibility, and engagement

COMMUNICATE DIRECTLY WITH YOUR TWITTER COMMUNITY

Helping internet users is a great way to attract followers as well by answering their questions, and enriching the conversation, you arouse interest, you can also take this opportunity to highlight the contents you offer on other social media platform. It's like you are standing in front of a podium delivering a speech to millions.

You can imagine how your tweets will be well analyzed and edited. Your brilliance is exposed. Each Twitter post or comment is top-notch and goes viral, giving you positive exposure.

LAUNCH ADVERTISING CAMPAIGNS ON TWITTER

Twitter gives the possibility of implementing "sponsored" content promotion campaigns. This allows you to meet two objectives:

The quest for followers with the possibility of targeting a population very precisely with specific interests,

The search for visibility through comments generates visibility and traffic to your website.

Knowing when to post is as crucial as what you post. Talk on the latest happenings in sport, politics, and other fields. You just need to keep marketing yourself on the platform. You are a commodity. You are a brand. This mindset is crucial to your community.

These days become conversations, which offer your brand an opportunity to interact with its audience organically. Make use of events and holidays.

Knowing what time to post is also important. For example, people are mostly present online in the afternoons on Sundays or at night during the week.

Friday night is another hit for your post. People are more online at that time, and this could increase more user engagement based on the subject matter.

ADDITIONAL TWITTER RESOURCES

20 Twitter Tricks to Make You Become an Expert in Tweeting By Jayson Demers
https://www.lifehack.org/articles/technology/20-twitter-tricks-make-you-become-expert-tweeting.html

Getting Standard -Twitter help center
https://www.help.twitter.com/en/twitter-guide/

Make a Website shares How to create a high impact Twitter profile that attracts followers
https://makeawebsitehub.com/perfect-twitter-profile/

How to make a twitter handle account
https://blog.wishpond.com/post/47480842552/how-to-make-a-twitter-handle-for-your-business-13

LET'S HAVE A CONVERSATION

Please Follow me at Twitter.com/CarlEReid

4.INSTAGRAM Is My Photo Journal

Photos | Fashion | Travel | Business

"Believe in your #selfie" -Unknown

Instagram.com was launched as a unique social networking platform that was based entirely on sharing photos and videos. This photo-sharing social networking app enables you to capture the best moments of your life, with your phone's camera or any other camera, and convert them into works of art.

Instagram is an American photo and video-sharing social networking service owned by Facebook, Inc. It was created by Kevin Systrom and Mike Krieger and launched in October 2010 on iOS. Posts can be shared publicly or with pre-approved followers. People can browse other content by tags and locations, and view trending content.

Instagram limits 30 hashtags per post. This includes cumulative hashtag count across the actual post captions, and any comments added.

NETWORKING BENEFITS

1. Accessible to Target (and Retarget) Your Audience.

2. Build up user-generated content.

3. Build a community that comes back time and time again.

4. More than <u>25 million businesses</u> running from agriculture, technology, fashion, transportation, entertainment are actively using Instagram to market to their target audience. Pictures move human beings. The platform allows the viewer to see for themselves what they are shopping for.

5. Online superstores like jumia, Jiji use Instagram ads for advertising their products since they sell physical goods. If you sell tangible assets, Instagram is the best online shop to shop for your wants.

6. It enables you to keep a tab on your audience through demographics, location, and interest of

your audience. Let your ads cover for what your audience is currently interested in. Once you know what your audience is shopping for, it allows you to prepare your advert well, either using videos or pictures that captivate your audience and make hem your prospective customers.

7. Instagram is free advertising!

8. Update your followers about sales and special promotions.

9. Build Connections with Like-Minded People.

10. Emotional Connection (Photos immediately convey emotional responses).

It helps to predict the number of people who possibly could become your customer because Instagram boasts over 800 million people every month and over 500 million logins every day. Spending your money and monitoring your ads will help to network, engage, and connect with your prospective buyers.

INSTAGRAM POWER NETWORKING TIPS

Below are six tips to help you engage people and start conversations with your fans and follower.

EMBRACE INSTAGRAM STORIES

From a marketing viewpoint, if you want to engage your followers, then you will need Instagram stories; they encourage interrelationship from everyone. The fact that they disappear after 24 hours forces you to post fresh content. This powers your consistency. Seeing that you have over 800 million people to attend to, you will want to be online, and at the same time, being active will help you level up on your consistency, especially when you have fewer views. Posting and reposting your Instagram stories helps you cover more audience and engagements. You must not be tired. The queue is long [with people] and you have millions to serve.

MENTION IN STORIES

When someone mentions you in their story, you will receive a notification. This is a sign that someone is interested in your topics posted and that's the best time to engage that person. Customers are like the wind blowing your way. Maximize the opportunity. Ensure you keep them or they will go to your competitors.

INSTAGRAM BUSINESS PROFILE

Switching to a business profile will give you access to more features like a contact button, Instagram Insights, and the ability to promote posts and add links to your Instagram Stories. Your personal Instagram profiles are much more different from your business profile.

POST SCHEDULE

By scheduling Instagram posts, you're assured of saving time with your marketing, giving you more time to focus on growing your account. The 'when' of every Instagram post is very important. Being on Instagram doesn't debar you from doing other things because you want to access over 500 million people, all you need to do is schedule your Instagram post and check your 'insights' for the number of engagements.

IGTV

This feature lets you post a video up to one hour though this is restricted to people with verified accounts. Many accounts are still limited to just ten minutes per video. There are dozens of ways to use IGTV. For job openings, product announcements, conferences, events.

IGTV has its app, available on Android and iOS. However, people can still watch IGTV from within the Instagram app. Similar to traditional television, IGTV features "channels," which are mostly the profiles of the video creators. Your channel is where people can watch the videos you've uploaded on IGTV.

Doesn't this look nice? Since you can't earn on your paid tv subscriptions, you can get prospective customers who are just watching your videos on IGTV becomes your customers. All you need is to make at least a 10min video and stay consistent with it.

Additional Instagram Resources

How to attract and engage followers
https://www.makeawebsitehub.com/get-followers-likes-instagram/

5 Ways To Authentically Network On Instagram – Forbes
https://www.forbes.com/sites/katetalbot/2017/12/15/5-ways-to-authentically-network-on-instagram/

Instagram Concept: Connecting People Over Common Interests by TK Kong
https://www.medium.com/@tkkong/instagram-concept-connecting-users-over-common-interests-ba99ee0603c4/

7 Tips for using Instagram for business
https://www.sendible.com/insights/7-tips-for-using-instagram-for-business/

The complete list of Instagram features for marketing expert
https://www.sproutsocial.com/insights/instagram-features/

10 ways to be more visible on Instagram
https://whatagraph.com/blog/articles/10-fresh-ways-to-be-more-visible-on-instagram

Let's Have A Conversation
We can connect at Instagram.com/CarlEReid

5.MEETUP Is My Face To Face

Special Interest Groups | In-Person Networking

The Meetup.com social networking portal enables you to find groups of like-minded people who have similar interests to you, near your locality (anywhere in the world). It also facilitates offline group meetings. You can become a part of such groups and their discussions. Meetup is a service used to startup online groups that host in-person events for people with a similar line of interests. The meetup was founded in 2002 by CEO Scott Heiferman and four co-founders.

Networking Benefits

1. Learn About Latest Industry Insights.
2. Put your ideas to the test.
3. Secure good opportunities.
4. Great way to bounce ideas off other people who can give you a fresh perspective.
5. Meet people, learn new things, find support, get out of their comfort zones, and pursue their passion.
6. Meet someone who shares your same interests.

7. It helps to make industry connections.
8. It enables you to prioritize your goal and achieve maximum output.
9. It helps you find a group based on your core interests and values.
10. It helps you to adapt and learn new relationships.
11. It helps you find new events and happenings within your circle.
12. It helps to make new friends and collaborations.
13. It helps to get the concrete and the latest information as a researcher.
14. Through connections and collaborations on meetup groups, you can extend your product and services to other areas while you are improving your brand in your local community.
15. You can also get freelancing jobs by advertising your brand and the abilities you possess.
16. On Meetup, you can exchange ideas and form an offline community or partnership that gives rise to a high level of impact and global recognition.
17. Joining meetup groups makes you a pleasant listener. This makes you very observant, helping you to learn and understand the needs of other people.

MEETUP POWER NETWORKING TIPS

1. ATTEND A PROFESSIONAL MEETUP

Attending the right meetups will instantly put you in the presence of professionals in your community.

2. CREATE YOUR MEETUP

Create it yourself (If you don't see a group for your interest). Be proactive. Connect with others in your community who share your interests.

3. CREATE YOUR BUSINESS PERSONAS

Creating your customer personas will give you a better idea of the kind of activities and events that each persona might be interested in.

Creating characters for your client will give you a better idea of the type of activities and events that each person might be interested in.

Say you own a gym. If one of your customers is a single woman who likes to hit the gym, you can't possibly mix her with couples who have children. These two groups do not have the same priorities or interests.

4. START A MEETUP TARGETED FOR EACH PERSONA

Create separate groups for each target character and promote events that give each group an impression of their ability to meet their specific needs. Give your group an attractive name that perfectly defines the audience you want to attract.

5.DO YOUR RESEARCH

Never join a meetup with no idea of what you want to get out of it. It's the same as doing customer or market research in business. Just as you check out your competitors before writing your business plan, you need to do thorough research on your Meetup group. This will allow you to know where you can exact your strength and get maximum benefits from it. Doing this will result in a more proactive and smooth conversation.

6. IT'S A MEETUP, NOT AN INTERVIEW

Meetups are informal. Expect to exchange pleasantries, share pieces of information and learn from each other. Use this time to establish a professional relationship and collaborations. No one can tell when you might need their expertise down the line.

7. BE FRIENDLY AND HELP OTHERS

People don't flow with strangers easily, and it takes time to build trust. Also, listen to the other person and don't judge them. If you have a lot more experience than they do, offer actionable advice, and follow up with them later. Everyone must start somewhere. 'Everyone can't be a teacher and there must be listeners called students. Listen more than you speak.

8. Be Accessible.

9. ASK FOR ADVICE

Asking questions is always an excellent way to show that you are actively listening to the other person. Consider being open and asking for advice that could be relevant to what the person brings to the table.

10. ENGAGE IN CONVERSATIONS

It can be unacceptable to interrupt, but sometimes the best way to break the ice is to insert yourself into the conversation. During a networking meetup, listen first. Then enter the conversation.

ADDITIONAL MEETUP RESOURCES

How to use Meetup to promote local business
https://www.business2community.com/social-media/how-to-use-meetup-com-to-promote-a-local-business-01331445

How to organize a successful meetup

https://www.mashable.com/2010/06/26/how-to-meetup

A YouTube video by Meetupon "3 Things every successful Meetup organizer should do."

https://www.youtube.com/watch?v=YRn5rPP950E

The Effectiveness Of Networking Through Meetup

https://www.compukol.com/the-effectiveness-of-networking-through-meetup

13 Tech Meetup Groups

https://skillcrush.com/blog/13-tech-meetup-groups-for-beginners

How to manage discussions on Meetup

https://help.meetup.com/hc/en-us/articles/360002863312-How-do-I-manage-discussions-

6. ALIGNABLE Is My Local Community
Referral Network | Forums | Q & A Updates

Alignable.com solves community needs by serving as a business directory. It is considered one of the most comprehensive business directories now in any town or city. It is a great way to foster new relationships.

It's designed to be a referral network, which is why they consider themselves a social network for local business owners and have developed the platform to help generate referrals. You can take interest in your business (locally) by creating an event or promotion. It started around 2014 and has millions of registered companies as members of the platform and has over 600 million US-based members.

CREATE A REFERRAL FLYER.

The referral flyer will auto-populate with companies you have given referrals. You can also share this over social media or add it to your website. This one-pager carries a lot of weight when it comes to showcasing businesses you support and collaborate with.

FORUM PARTICIPATION

Participating in the Ask and Learn forum allows you to poll potential customers and discover insights on a topic you might not typically be able to access a significant data set. Maybe you want to deliver a speech at a hotel or organize an outdoor event where the number of people in attendance cannot be determined. The Forum is an excellent platform to read, share your views or check the level of interest on a specific topic. Participating in forum discussions allows you to have committed followers who share your interest on that particular subject.

SET UP INSTANT GROUP BUSINESS MESSAGING

You can now chat in real-time with all your business contacts. You can add up to twenty people, whether they are Alignable members or not. Create a group by entering their names or email addresses. Simply write a message and click send. This is a useful tool to launch a business in a new market or stay in front of potential consumers. The business messaging groups allow your business contact to see the other promising side of your business, perhaps through innovations and different marketing strategies. With this group, you can pitch your business idea from time to time to convince your audience to prefer your product and services to others. Your audience can view your stock through images posted and ask questions directly about your services. Keep your audience satisfied. Check their interest for newer updates on your products and services. By doing this, you will be surprised at the results.

PROVIDE REFERRALS

Refer to your favorite businesses. It's like getting a card in the mail. Take 5 minutes and craft a sincere and thoughtful referral for your clients and the best local haunts. It will help position you as a thought leader in your local business community. Referrals are critical in business. Your addiction to a product is a product of referral. Someone at a point in time told you about the product, and you tested the product or services, you found it helpful and it became one of the products or services you can't do without. If you have a quality product or service, each satisfied customer is sure to refer more buyers.

POST UPDATES

There is something to be said for sharing content in a storytelling fashion, especially when it is useful to other business owners. Using a compelling story is very important. You are pitching an idea to your prospective customers who are emotionally designed to respond base on how it aligns with their story or something they've perceived before. For example, you know a family household in financial need. You want help by engaging financial contributors. You write a story about the family's current situation, along with any special medical conditions or medications the parents or children in the family take? Suppose you emphasize just one dollar can save a life? People become emotionally connected to those types of stories. Then you see your followers sharing your compelling story. This the viral power of social media in action.

What about keeping people in suspense? Post an incomplete or cliff hanger statement. People are inquisitive. They want to know the rest of the story. What about using idioms to explain your points. What about using rhymes and poems. This will help people engage more with LIKEs or comments.

If you are already publishing content in the form of blog posts or case studies, it is a great place to share this content to drive more people to your website.

Networking Benefits

1. Link up local businesses to collaborate and communicate to increase their customer base.

ALIGNABLE POWER NETWORKING TIPS

1. SETUP YOUR PROFILE
   Your photo will appear when you comment, communicate and answer questions in the Forum. Set aside the time to deliberately depict your business and select the tags that best portray what you do and who you want to work with. This is a great chance to clearly define what you offer, Set up your profile before you connect to people, or invite people to join you on Alignable.

2. LEARN THE PLATFORM
   Set aside a little time to figure out how the framework functions. You can monitor your network, give and get proposals, and take an interest in the Forum by addressing questions presented by the individual members.

3. ANSWER QUESTIONS
   Alignable will send questions from people who are in your field. You do not have to answer every question Alignable sends you. If you feel you have a definite answer, then go for it.
   Be given to understand that this is not the place to lure people to work with you or to sell your product.

4. Grow your community

5. Use the grow my network page.

6. Add details about your customers on your profile.

7. Add your product and services.

8. Update your profile.

9. Use align about for any further questions on the platform.

ADDITIONAL ALIGNABLE RESOURCES

where are referral cards, and how do I use them.

https://support.alignable.com/hc/en-us/articles/360006855772-What-are-referral-cards-and-how-do-I-use-them-Referral-Cards-FAQ-

How to create a group chat on Alignable

https://support.alignable.com/hc/en-us/articles/360022212311-How-do-I-create-a-Group-Chat-

How do I edit the ideal customer section on the profile section

https://support.alignable.com/hc/en-us/articles/360001070952-How-Do-I-Edit-the-Ideal-Customer-Section-of-My-Profile-

LET'S HAVE A CONVERSATION

Let's connect on Alignable, so I can refer local clients to you Alignable.com/new-rochelle-ny/savvy-intrapreneur

7. BUMBLE BIZZ IS MY QUICK CONNECTION

CAREER | BUSINESS | DATING | FRIENDSHIP

Bumble.com is the first app of its kind to bring dating, friend-finding, and career-building into a single social networking platform. Bumble Bizz is the place to find positive and empowering professional connections

NETWORKING BENEFITS

1. Networking shouldn't feel so hard or, worse, uncomfortable. Bumble made it so you can make life-changing connections at your own pace, on your own terms.
2. Get connected to real, verified professionals.
3. Showcase your portfolios or other work you've done.
4. Networking directly with other business owners in your area who are looking for mentors/mentees.

BUMBLE BIZZ POWER NETWORKING TIPS

PROFILE SETUP

There's more to communicate when you're networking, so there is more room to tell your professional story.

What goes into a Bumble Bizz profile?

- Headline

- Experience

- About

- Use your photo to complete your story

SHARE THE WHO AND THE WHY, NOT THE WHAT

People do want to know why you started your company or why you do what you do. They want to get to know who you are versus what you're doing. You are your differentiating factor. There's no room for you to build your brand the same way someone else is building theirs. There's only room for you to do it your way. Own your voice - Amy Jo Martin.

GET A MENTOR TO MEET WITH YOU

Seven tips that will not only help you ask a mentor out for a coffee and conversation but also improve the chances that they will say yes.

1. Show interest in their work

2. Exercise your elevator pitch (what do you hope to get out of this meeting)

3. Don't mention the 'Mentor' word.

4. Keep it short and sweet.

5. Get straight to the point.

ADDITIONAL BUMBLE BIZZ RESOURCES

5 Tips for Your Bumble Bizz Coffee Meet Up
https://bumble.com/the-buzz/coffee-network-meet-up-etiquette/

How to Create a Bumble Bizz Profile That Will Get You Noticed.
https://bumble.com/the-buzz/how-to-get-noticed-on-bumble-bizz-profile/

An article titled 'What Makes a Good Bumble Bizz Profile?' By Bumble.com
https://bumble.com/the-buzz/bumble-bizz-profile-best-practices/

An article titled ' to Write Bumble Bizz Headline That People will Actually Notice' by Bumble.com
https://bumble.com/the-buzz/how-to-write-a-bumble-bizz-headline-that-people-will-actually-notice/

A blog post written by Destiny Lalane titled "A Competitive Way To Network and Find Clients With Bumble Bizz"
https://www.destinylalane.com/blog/networking-apps

8. WHATSAPP IS MY GROUP MESSAGE CENTER

INDIVIDUAL AND GROUP MESSAGING | CALLS

Despite having been acquired by Facebook in 2014, it has been able to capture the imagination of millions of people across the world by giving them the ability to communicate and share instantly with individuals and groups. The WhatsApp call feature is just the icing on the cake!

WhatsApp uses your phone's cellular or Wi-Fi connection to facilitate messaging and voice calling to nearly anyone on the planet, alone or in a group, and is especially excellent for families and small collaborative workgroups. The app lets you make calls and send and receive messages, documents, photos, and videos. WhatsApp is completely free — no fees or subscriptions — because it uses your phone's 4G, 3G, 2G, EDGE, or Wi-Fi connection instead of your cell plan's voice minutes or text plan, and if you are connected via Wi-Fi, it won't eat into your data plan, either. Its popularity is sustained by its support for worldwide free calling, even if the people chatting are not in the same country.

NETWORKING BENEFITS

1. Messaging privately and securely.

2. WhatsApp is completely free for use.

3. Video Calling lets you video call your contacts using WhatsApp.

4. WhatsApp offers direct communication between family and friends, customers, and business representatives through short but helpful messages.

5. WhatsApp is a magnificent tool for endorsing new varieties of your products or offers that are available on discounted rates.

6. It shows that your message is sent or not, and the receiver has received or reads the message.

7. WhatsApp started providing end-to-end encryption feature, which makes your WhatsApp communication highly secure.

WHATSAPP POWER NETWORKING TIPS

WHATSAPP GROUP

Keep in touch with groups of people that matter the most, like your family, coworkers, and customers.

With group chats, you can share messages, photos and videos with up to 256 people at once and you can also name your group, mute or customize notifications and more.

VOICE AND VIDEO CALLS (SPEAK FREELY)

With voice calls, you can talk to your friends and family for free, even if they are a million miles away. And with video calls, you can have a face to face conversations for when voice or text isn't enough.

WHATSAPP STATUS/STORY

This feature is to share free content with your WhatsApp contacts. The content you share can only last 24 hours, after which the picture or video disappears.

AUTO RESPOND (BUSINESS ACCOUNT ONLY)

With Automated Responses, you're able to set an away message when you're unable to respond immediately to your customers and let them know when they can expect a response.

CREATE BROADCAST LIST

Generate lists related to specific topics, then disperse your message or content, it's a tool designed to increase engagement, links can be included.

CREATE OFFERS AND PROMOTIONS

Looking for innovative ways to create new offers? WhatsApp may be just what you need. And it can be used to direct people to promotions on other platforms.

KNOW YOUR TARGET AUDIENCE

QUALITY CONTENT MUST BE MAINTAIN

ADDITIONAL WHATSAPP RESOURCES

How to Use WhatsApp: A Complete Guide to Getting Started https://www.digitaltrends.com/mobile/how-to-use-whatsapp/

How to use WhatsApp: Tips, Tricks and more| Tom's guide https://www.tomsguide.com/us/pictures-story/528-whatsapp-how-to-user-guide.html/

Configuring your privacy settings – WhatsApp FAQ https://faq.whatsapp.com/android/23225461/

How to run a successful WhatsApp Group – Forbes by Paul Armstrong https://www.forbes.com/sites/paularmstrongtech/2018/04/29/how-to-run-a-successful-whatsapp-group/#6355a26c6364/

How to Use WhatsApp Responsibly-WhatsApp FAQ https://faq.whatsapp.com/en/android/26000240/?category=5245250/

How to Use WhatsApp (with Pictures)- WikiHow https://www.wikihow.com/Use-WhatsApp/

9.YOUTUBE IS MY LEARNING LIBRARY

LEARN NEW SKILLS | SUBSCRIBE TO TOPIC CHANNELS | ENTERTAINMENT

"Knowledge is power. Information is liberating. Education is the premise of progress, in every society, in every family." – Kofi Annan

YouTube is THE LARGEST encyclopedia in the world. Good or bad you can learn how to do anything by typing "How to do . . . anything"

YouTube allows registered people to upload, view, rate, share, add to playlists, report and subscribe to content posted by other people.

Video blogging, educational videos, short original video, funny videos, Tv shows, movie trailers can be found on YouTube. People can upload content.

YouTube and some content creators earn advertising revenue from Adsense, a Google program for placing Ads.

The 3 Main Types of YouTube Videos

The majority of the videos on YouTube fall into one of the following categories:

1. Educational videos (helpful how-to advice about a specific topic).

2. Inspirational videos (pulls on your heartstrings and inspires you to take action).

3. Entertaining videos (captures your attention, meant for fun).

RESEARCH LINKS
https://www.thinkific.com/blog/youtube-video-marketing-guide/

https://digitalmarketinginstitute.com/en-us/blog/the-importance-of-video-marketing

NETWORKING BENEFITS

1. YouTube is your best channel to use for video marketing.
2. GENERATE LEADS - No matter who your audience is, they are likely using YouTube, YouTube is the second most visited site. Your potential for exposure is unlimited.

3. GAIN RETURN ON INVESTMENT (ROI) FROM MULTIPLE VIDEO MARKETING CHANNELS - When you create a video to market your business, you need to see ROI. Simply put, creating and posting YouTube videos is a powerful asset to any digital marketing strategy.

4. REACH WORLDWIDE AUDIENCES - YouTube is available and is used worldwide, accessible anywhere, on every device.

5. CONTENT CAN BE MONETIZED

YOUTUBE POWER NETWORKING TIPS

OPTIMIZE YOUR INTRODUCTION

The theme song can be skipped. Get to the point very quickly. Explain within the first 10 seconds of your video what you'll be discussing and how it helps.

Benefit first. This way, your audience can self-filter.

CHOOSE A GREAT VIDEO TITLE

Do well to perform research on your tile. Are you considering how your target audience will find your content?

Go with a title for your video that reflects what your audience would actually type into the YouTube search box. Natural language and organic keywords will get you more exposure.

KEEP IT SHORT AND SWEET

It's straightforward to get someone to click your video. Getting them to engage is not as easy. The best advice is to make your video short and precise, full of information.

USE A CALL TO ACTION

Ending your video with a call to action will create more chances of getting more engagement. You can choose from a variety of measures, depending on your goal.

- Ask viewers to subscribe
- To get them to your website, ask them to follow a link in your description.
- To get feedback to ask them to leave a comment

ADDITIONAL YOUTUBE RESOURCES

YouTube video by Roberto Blake on "How to Grow a Small YouTube Channel"
https://www.youtube.com/watch?v=V9XA9pLuHIc/

A blog article by Adam Coombs on "21 Tips on How to Get More Views on YouTube for free."

https://unamo.com/blog/social/21-tips-on-how-to-get-more-views-on-youtube-for-free

How to create a YouTube channel in 3 simple steps-Buffer

https://buffer.com/library/create-a-youtube-channel

10. QUORA IS MY EXPERT

SOCIAL Q & A | EXPERT FORUMS | PROFESSIONAL CONNECTIONS

Quora is a continually growing user-generated collection of questions and answers. All the questions and answers are created, edited, and organized by the people who use them. While many people use Quora as a resource for information, research, and general interest, some use Quora to Add and build their social network.

RESEARCH LINKS
https://www.adweek.com/digital/how-to-use-quora-a-comprehensive-guide/

NETWORKING BENEFITS

1. Quora allows you to connect with people that are relevant to your industry.
2. Quora allows you to link your webpage by answering questions, therefore use your most useful and informative blog posts and use them wisely. If your answers get noticed, you will see a rapid change in your traffic.

QUORA POWER NETWORKING TIPS

QOURA PROFILE

The profile is the personal portal to everything on Quora. You can upload your picture and follow other people on the platform. Fill out the information needed to complete your profile. Also, add a headline to your profile. A headline is like a short bio.

ACTIVITY FEED

Activity feed has recent activity about the contents that interest you. What's on your feed is dependent on the number of topics you follow or search

PICK THE RIGHT QUESTION AND ANSWERS

Finding a question is easy; finding the right question is incredibly difficult.
Instead focus on:

- Number of views should be high.
- The post should have engagements (Followers).
- Keep it within your field of work/ interest.

ANSWER QUESTIONS

Provide valuable thought and ideas before dropping your links. People want you to prove that you can provide value before they blindly lead you.
If all you're saying is, "Look at my things! Click over to my site" they are not going to follow you or upvote you.

ADD EXTRAS TO YOUR ANSWER

Few things you can do to help gain momentum.

- Add an image to your answer.
- Use sources (link, footnotes).
- Become a thought leader in a particular field.

BE ACTIVE

After setting up your account, log in to Quora, and check out the contents. Check various questions and answer, follow people who engage or join the discussions, and upvote their updates. Even if your account is new, upvotes appear on the public profile, so it's an excellent way to show that there's some activity going on.

COMMUNICATE WITH YOUR CUSTOMERS

Effective communication with your customers is one of the exceptional benefits of being active on Quora. Personally answering topics may give you an edge. It may win over new customers.

DISPLAY PROFESSIONAL TITLES TO SETUP AUTHORITY

Quora's community provides rich and pertinent answers to the things people are looking for, curious, or interested about. This ensures that the center of attention of the website will always be satisfying and catering for the interest of the user and followers.

The competition among answers motivates only the most well informed and learned people to participate. For this reason, many display their business affiliation and professional title as a sign of trust in their response

UPVOTE AND DOWNVOTE

Answers can be ranked based on how relevant the answer is. This is put in place to help maintaining the standard of contents posted online.

QOURA DIGEST

Quora Digest is an email newsletter sent by Quora to registered members who have viewed answers to specific questions on Quora's website. The content of the emails looks different based on the topics Quora has found each member to be most interested in.

ADDITIONAL QUORA RESOURCES

An article by Morgan Timm on "Quora Marketing 101: How to Get Traffic From Quora"
https://teachable.com/blog/quora-marketing/

Marketing with Quora: What is it and why You should care
https://www.precisionmarketinggroup.com/blog/quora-for-new-users/

Quora Features and Advantages by Manmohan Yadav
https://pitechnologies.org/pitechblog/Quora-Features-and-Advantages/191/

Using Quora for business purpose by Martin Luenendonk
https://www.cleverism.com/using-quora-business-purposes/

A YouTube video tutorial titled" Sign Up for Quora & Setup Your Profile" by Exprance
https://www.youtube.com/watch?v=KrN090_HQKE/

A HubSpot article written by Brian Whalley titled "What is Quora? A Marketer's Guide to the Most Underrated Platform of 2020" https://blog.hubspot.com/blog/tabid/6307/bid/9167/a-marketer-s-guide-to-quora.aspx

An Adweek article written by Kelsey Blair titled "How to Use Quora: A comprehensive Guide." https://www.adweek.com/digital/how-to-use-quora-a-comprehensive-guide/

LET'S HAVE A CONVERSATION

Let's connect on Quora
Quora.com/profile/Carl-E-Reid-1

11. BONUS: ZOOM IS MY VIDEO CONFERENCE MEETING
VIDEO CONFERENCE | WEBINARS | GROUP CONFERENCE CALLS | PRESENTATIONS

Zoom.us is a Free App that allows both video conferencing and telephone conference calls

Certain world events recently propelled Zoom Video Communications as the social distancing tool of choice. It is a videoconferencing company in San Jose, California. Its iOS app became the top free download in Apple's App Store.

Zoom is Built For 21st Century Teams And Community Building

ZOOM IS BUILT FOR 21ST CENTURY TEAM AND COMMUNITY BUILDING

HD Video and Audio
Bring HD video and audio to your meetings with support for up to 1000 video participants and 49 videos on screen.

Team Chat
Chat with groups, searchable history, integrated file sharing and 10-year archive. Easily escalate into 1:1 or group calls.

91

Built-in Collaboration Tools

Multiple participants can share their screens simultaneously and co-annotate for a more interactive meeting.

Meet Securely

End-to-end encryption for all meetings, role-based user security, password protection, waiting rooms, and place attendee on hold.

Streamlined Calendaring

Support scheduling or starting meetings from Outlook, Gmail, or iCal.

Recording and Transcripts

Record your meetings locally or to the cloud, with searchable transcripts.

Free Zoom Version Features

- Host up to 100 participants
- Unlimited 1 to 1 meetings
- 40 mins limit on group meetings
- Unlimited number of meetings

Zoom Training Services

Zoom.us/livetraining

Zoom Featured Events

Zoom.us/events

ADDITIONAL MEETING RESOURCES

WhenAvailable.com allows you to find a day and time that works best for everyone to gather. Scheduling a video conference, family reunions, book club meeting, or a men / ladies' night out has never been simpler. Find the best possible time for your event based on input from everyone you invite.

FreeConferenceCall.com - If you're not quite ready for video conferencing, FreeConferenceCall.com provides you with a personal telephone conference call number you can share with family, friends and business associates. Up to 99 people can join a conference call. Record conference calls for essential meetings to eliminate someone having to take minutes. You can transcribe minutes later and / or provide recording to people who missed the meeting.

12. Bonus: Cell Phone Is My Communication Hub

Enhance Your Brand With Voicemail

- **Incoming message** – When you leave a voicemail message, be brief with positive energy that motivates people to call you back. Identify yourself [don't say "it's me"]. Share your telephone number slowly, in case the receiver wants to write it down. Date stamp your message by saying the day, date and time, being mindful of time zones (EST, PST etc.). Repeat your telephone number slowly. Never assume anyone has your telephone number. Technology has a nasty habit of losing contact information all the time.

- **Outgoing message** – Record a personalized, professional message with confident high energy that lathers callers up to want to leave you a message.

Mobile Library

- Listen to audio books, while performing other activities (i.e. driving, computer activity etc.).
- Learn a new skill or language.
- Download Kindle reader to read books.

Meetings and Conferences

Perform information sharing, learning exchanges and team building by coordinating conference calls, video conferences, group chats.

Text Message Etiquette

- Consider your audience. ...
- Communicate clearly. ...
- Responding promptly maintains your networking credibility.
- Use symbols and emojis appropriately. Consider each phone provider may convert emojis to indiscernible characters or they may not display at all.
- Do not be verbose. Send short messages. Consider the time of each person you text.
- Be patient. People have different texting habits. Their response may not be immediate.
- Know when to end the conversation
- After four (4) text message volleys back and forth, the conversation should be continued with a phone call. This expedites and provides

clarification with any personal or business process.

- Ping your contacts, via text message, to stay in touch. Use holidays, birthdays, special occasions and informative article shares as opportunities to keep your name in front of people. Have you heard the saying "out of sight. Out of mind."
- Add your full name as the signature to your text message. This way anyone you text **always** knows with whom they are communicating. This elevates and enhances your brand too.

TREAT CONTACTS LIKE GOLD

People connections are the life blood for achieving anything

- Back-Up Your Phone Contacts. It could be a bad assumption that your cell phone provider is backing up your contacts. Go beyond turning "On" your phone setting to back up contacts. Have a backup copy on your computer or another backup device (i.e. thumb drive, external drive, vaulting service etc.).
- Print a hard copy of your contacts. Technology has a nasty habit of failing or being unavailable when we most need it.

- Protect your contacts. When connecting contacts, ONLY share contact information with permission.

13. BONUS: EMAIL IS MY INTEGRATED SOCIAL CENTER

Social media is an ingredient, not an entree. This means your email system is your central communication center to be integrated with your social messaging.

Here are 4 key reasons why email will always rule:

1. More people still use email over social media.

2. Email can be personalized.

3. Email is algorithm free. Many social media sites have nebulous programming rules for how posts are displayed. With email, what you see is what you get.

4. You have total control over your email communications. You are in the driver seat with when, how and what you will share with your email contacts.

10 WAYS TO INCREASE YOUR EMAIL SOCIALIZATION BRAND

Just like TV commercials leverage email to keep your name in front people in your network. Below are tips to enhance your email engagements for effective communication.

1. Write emails as brief and concise as possible. If you need help saying MORE with less words, I recommend reading "Elements Of Style" by William Strunk JR. and E.B. White. It's about 60 pages, but packed with powerful tips on communicating succinctly.
2. To increase productivity create filters so emails from people you know only get placed in your Primary inbox. All other emails should be filtered into other secondary inbox folders.
3. Create an email signature that contains contact information and links to your social media sites. This allows you to be where your contacts hangout. The more convenient you make it for people to call you, the faster they will call.
4. To increase emails getting opened and read, write provocative, catchy "Subject" lines.
5. CHANGE the "Subject" line when the topic discussion changes. To eliminate your email being deleted without being read, Do not reply to old emails and keep the same Subject from an old conversation. New Topic = New Subject.

6. Be mindful of email habits. Everyone has different habits when it comes to reading and replying to email. Yes, you are a professional with a "do it now" mindset. So, you reply to an email at 2:00AM Saturday to get it off your plate. Where do you think your reply email will be located for viewing, if your email reader(s) wait until Monday to read email and they received 178 more emails after you replied? Your reply email will sit at the bottom of 178 other emails.

7. To increase email open, read and respond rate, ALWAYS send email to the reader's local time zones during their business or daylight hours. If you're in New York City sending an email at 10AM TODAY to a person in Sidney Australia with their local time being 1:00AM TOMORROW, what are the chances of them immediately opening your email?

8. Never write and send an email when you are angry. (see article in the "Additional Resources" section below.)

9. Do not use Text message slang abbreviations or emojis.

10. Be prudent using the BCC (blind carbon copy) email address area. It can build trust with relationships or destroy relationships.

11. Share opportunities and articles with people in your network. This builds trust while enhancing your brand. It also keeps your name on top of a

person's mind when they need your service or product.

ADDITIONAL RESOURCES FOR EMAIL SOCIAL MESSAGING INTEGRATION

To stay in compliance with the 2003 CAN-SPAM Act Regulations and prevent your email address from being "blacklisted" by email providers, consider using distribution mailing lists that include 2-way communication discussion groups. This allows you to drive the conversations by creating special interest groups by using email. This is your own personal group you can manage or assign other people to manage the discussion groups.

MailChimp.com | ConstantContact.com and my favorite is ElectricEmbers.coop
The original LISTSERV Email List Management Software is L-Soft http://www.lsoft.com

6 Creative Ways to Integrate Social Media and Email Marketing by Jimmy Daly - Follow on Twitter @jimmy_daly.
https://buffer.com/resources/social-media-email-marketing

Tools that integrate with Gmail to discover detailed information about your email contacts for enhanced collaborations and have productive conversations. https://www.leadgibbon.com/blog/rapportive-alternatives/

The simplest way to schedule an email reminder https://www.FollowUpThen.com

19 Tips to Write Catchy Email Subject Lines by Olivia Allen Follow on Twitter: @o_allen954 blog.hubspot.com/marketing/improve-your-email-subject-line

Time Zone Converter Tool
https://www.timeanddate.com/worldclock/converter.html

Schedule Gmail Email For Local Time Zones
Using computer desktop web browser, follow these steps:

1. Compose a new email.
2. Click the triangle next to the blue "Send" button.
3. Select one of the suggested times or click "Pick date & time" to customize precisely when you want the message to go out.
4. Click "Schedule send".

5 Reputation Saving Tips When Writing Angry Emails
By Carl E. Reid
https://www.linkedin.com/pulse/5-reputation-saving-tips-when-writing-angry-emails-carl-e-reid-csi

Suggested book for succinct email writing is *The Elements Of Style* by William Strunk, Jr. and E.B. White. Teaches how to say more with fewer words.

SOCIAL MEDIA SECURITY

Just because you login to a social site with custom security settings, that does not necessarily mean your shared posts are viewable to only your selected community of friends and family.

Protect your integrity and reputation. Trust, but VERIFY before you share anything. Google is your friend to verify and fact check. Call a few people in your warm, trusted network to run received information by them.

- Use pass phrases instead of passwords. The goal is to thwart hackers with a pass phrase, which easy to remember but hard to crack the sequence. Mix lowercase and uppercase letters with special characters. The longer it is, the more secure it will be.
- Use a unique pass phrases for each of your social media accounts.
- Don't save passwords in your web browser.
- Store your login IDs and passwords in a password protected document you keep only on your computer. Do not store on your phone.
- Set up your security answers. This option is available for most social media sites.
- Password protect your mobile devices, if you have Apps installed.

- Be selective with friend requests. If you don't know the person, don't accept their connection request. It might be a fake account.
- Never click on a link sent from unknown people. Text or call a known person to confirm they REALLY sent you the web link. Trust, but VERIFY. Social media accounts are regularly hacked. Look out for language, content and misspellings that do not sound like something your friend would post.
- Be careful about what you share. Don't reveal sensitive personal information (i.e. home address, financial information, phone number). The more you post the easier it is to have your identity stolen.
- READ privacy policies and terms of service (TOS) agreements on all your social media real estate. Then adjust your privacy settings according to who you want to view your posts.
- Protect computer access with antivirus software. Make sure your web browser, operating system and application software are updated to the latest version.
- Embrace 2 step Login authentication. This works very well because you will receive either an email or text message to confirm you are the person that logged in to your social media account. This is an excellent way to thwart

hackers, should they obtain your login ID and password.

- Logoff when you're finished socializing in each site.

ADDITIONAL SECURITY RESOURCES

Fact Checking Websites (Check multiple sources)

https://Factcheck.org

Washington Post Fact Checker
https://www.washingtonpost.com/news/fact-checker

https://FlackCheck.org

https://Hoax-Slayer.com

https://Politifact.com

https://Snopes.com

https://ThatsFake.com

https://ThatsNonsense.com

Pass Phrase Generators

Rempe.us/diceware/#eff

Fourmilab.ch/javascrypt/pass_phrase.html

HEALTH AND WELLNESS WORK LIFE BALANCE

One day while riding on the train to meet with a client, I realized I left my cell phone home. At first, I was annoyed and angry at myself. I felt disconnected and mentally naked due to not having access to contacts, information and social networks which allow me to perform as a technology consultant.

Then I took a breath and mentally stepped back. I talked myself into turning this into an opportunity. This allowed me to accept being disconnected as an experiment for the rest of the day. . . "Let's see how the day goes" I said to myself.

It was one of THE BEST decisions I made. I felt refreshed at the end of the day. Since that experience I designated Tuesday as my cell phone disconnect day. I check my cell phone social media 15 minutes in the morning, afternoon and before I go to bed. I respond to email throughout the day from my computer, but No social media activity.

This may not work for you. I will share some suggestions to allow a modified social media wellness disconnection.

Take Extended Breaks

Consider going without social media for a month, 1-week vacation, 1 day or just 2 hours per day? I can tell you from personal experience what a difference it makes in taking back your life, without social media.

Find New Hobbies Or Activities

Look for hobbies that builds confidence and provides new perspectives. Consider taking up new activities like cooking, book club readings, biking, long walks, board games etc.

Treat People With Respect

Words on a screen are still attached to a human person on the other side.

Appreciate The Value Of Real-Life Interactions

People appreciate knowing their friendship is valued beyond social media. With meaningful friendships, it's quality, not quantity that matters.

Limit Social Media Usage

Avoid checking social media constantly to the point it rules your daily life. Check it 10 minutes in the morning, afternoon and maybe before bed.

ADDITIONAL BREAK RESOURCES

100+ Things To Do Instead Of Social Media
BY Michelle Schroeder-Gardner

https://www.makingsenseofcents.com/2020/02/things-to-do-instead-of-social-media.html

Here's How to Do a Social Media Detox the Right Way - By Andra Chantim

https://www.goodhousekeeping.com/life/g30681374/social-media-detox-tips

Vanity Domain Be Thy Name

Have you Googled yourself lately? Googling yourself is not vain -- it's smart. The search results from Googling your name become your online business card. Therefore, you should be aware of what comes up when someone enters your name into that magnifying glass called Google.

Acquiring a domain with your FrstNameLastName.com is a smart, inexpensive $20 investment in developing your brand reputation.

What stands out better on a business card?

LinkedIn.com/in/jerrypsmith
(you marketing LinkedIn's brand)
OR
www.JerryPSmith.com
(You marketing your own brand)

Vanity Domain Name Benefits

Control after meeting conversation - These days, it is a safe bet anyone who can, will search for you online after meeting you. Acquiring your own domain name that is same as you your full name [YourFirstNameLastName.com], allows you to control what a person sees when they check you out.

Elevate YOU As A Brand – It's your link, so why would you promote another company's brand name in your short links when you can use your own. By using a branded link, your brand name will be seen more, even when you share content produced by other people.

Increased Trust – The fact that you are willing to attach your brand name to the content you're sharing tells followers that your link won't redirect them to spam or phishing sites. The content you are linking them to is relevant and consistent with your personal brand.

Link Management Control – Having your custom branded domain allows control over where you direct people. You can delete them, redirect the destination or edit the description as your business requirements change.

Make It Easy To Remember YOU – Vanity domains are real words that people can understand and read. This means that your links are more memorable and pronounceable. Instead of a generic link that people will usually scan over, your link can be easily read – giving your message another chance to be consumed.

Social Media Scheduling Tools

Let's face it. Your time is valuable and limited. When it comes to social media the question to ask yourself is "Do I want to be in the social media business or do I want to spend my time working on my business?".

Below are tools to make your socializing life easier.

Buffer.com is a software application for web and mobile that lets you schedule content to Twitter, Facebook, Pinterest, Instagram and LinkedIn from a single dashboard. Buffer can be used by anyone looking for a simple and easy way to schedule social media updates.

TweetDeck.com is a social media dashboard application for managing Twitter accounts only. Twitter acquired TweetDeck in 2011. So Twitter is integrated into the TweetDeck interface. TweetDeck can be used by anyone who wants a completely free tool that allows basic scheduling of posts on Twitter.

Sendible.com is an all-in-one social media management tool designed to help solopreneurs and agencies manage and amplify their brands. Posts are stored in the interactive calendar. If you need to modify post scheduling, you can quickly move content around. Sendible can be used by Bloggers, marketers and agencies.

AgoraPulse.com is another all-in-one social media management tool that includes excellent scheduling functionality. AgoraPulse's feature-rich publishing options allow you to pre-schedule content posts in advance. AgoraPulse can be used by marketers and agencies that require a single tool to manage all their social media needs.

SocialBee.io is a social media management tool that that also includes competitor research feature. Entrepreneurs, freelancers and marketing agencies can use SocialBee.

MeetEdgar.com is a purpose-built social media scheduling and automation tool that makes it a breeze to publish on Facebook, Twitter, Instagram, and LinkedIn. Twitter's rules prohibit reposting the same content. So MeetEdgar has a 'Variations' tool that allows you to reshare the same content with a unique twist. MeetEdgar can be used by bloggers and businesses requiring a dedicated scheduling tool with straight forward pricing that includes extensive features.

SmarterQueue.com is a purpose-built tool for scheduling your social media updates on Facebook, Twitter, LinkedIn, Instagram, and Pinterest. It uses categories to manage different content like blog posts, questions, quotes and self-branding. SmarterQueue can be used by businesses and agencies requiring a robust social media scheduling tool.

SOCIAL MEDIA GLOSSARY OF TERMS

- A -

AMA (ask me anything) – Q&A sessions often hosted on Facebook, Instagram or Twitter for various purposes such as audience engagement and product updates.

Algorithms – social media platforms use algorithms to ensure people are alerted to the most relevant content using certain demographic predictions. This means that new content may be pushed below content which is deemed more relevant to the user.

Application Programming Interface (API) – a set of methods that allows different pieces of software to communicate with each other. For example, social media scheduling and reporting tools such as Hootsuite use API to integrate with social media accounts and publish posts or collect data.

Attribution – the process of identifying a set of user actions ("events" or "touchpoints") that contribute in some manner to the desired outcome, and then assigning a value to each of these events.

Automation – there are many tools available to automate social media marketing, such as Hootsuite. However, make sure you always take the time to engage directly with your audience and don't rely too heavily on automation.

Avatar – in social media, an Avatar is a picture or graphic used to represent you. Businesses frequently use a logo as their avatar on company pages and profiles.

- B -

Behavior segmentation – the process where a brand targets its online audience based on behaviors like attitude, knowledge, use frequency and sentiment towards them.

Bio – a short description usually at the top of a profile on a social network that offers a short description of the owner of the account.

Bitmoji – a mobile application that allows you to create your own personalized cartoon avatar which can be used on various social networks or messaging services such as Snapchat.

Blogs – a web content publishing platform that allows a user to post content which may include commentaries, news or views. Blogging platforms include Blogger and WordPress, and blogs are indexed promptly by search engines. Read more about blogging for lead generation.

Boosted posts – without paid advertising, only 0.02% of posts are seen. This means that Facebook content from brands is often 'boosted' to increase its visibility. This involves a budget, which sends the content to a selected audience based on demographical and behavioral data.

- C -

Canvas ads – canvas ads are Facebook's most immersive form of advertising, designed to help businesses tell stories and show products on mobile devices, in a dynamic way. The full-screen advertising is hosted on Facebook, rather than on an outside page, which lowers the likelihood of user drop-offs.

Caption – a short description of an image on Instagram underneath the image offering more details about the context of the picture and can include tags and hashtags.

Chat – live/real-time text-based communication between two or more people using a service available on the Internet.

Circles – or rather Google Circles, are a feature of Google+. A Circle is a way of categorizing or grouping people based on the relationship you have with them. People you add on Google+ can be added as friends, family, acquaintances, or you can add people to follow.

Clickbait – online content created to attract visitors and determine them to click on a link.

Clickthrough rate – the number of people that clicked on a link divided by the number of people that saw the link.

Community management – the management of a brand's relationship with its community of customers, prospects, fans, advocates and other people that interact with the brand online.

Connections – connections are people you connect with on LinkedIn. Connections are similar to Facebook friends but are more likely to be made with people you have worked with, or would like to do business with, rather than friends or family members.

Content curation – the process of gathering information related to a topic with the intent of publishing it.

- D -

Dark posts – dark posts were once an invisible advertising tactic that brands used to target a specific set of people. Facebook announced that it plans to disclose what groups and companies paid for ads on its platform, with any ads running on Facebook being readily viewable by everyone. More on dark posts here and here.

Delicious – a social bookmarking web service for discovering, storing and sharing web bookmarks. It allows you to share bookmarks to make others aware of the content that you find interesting. Delicious bookmarks are placed on the Delicious site, and can be a way to increase the reach of your great content.

Digg – Digg is a news aggregator with a curated front page that selects stories with topics that vary widely from trending political issues to science to viral stories and anything in between. It allows you to share content that may include news, videos or pictures. People rate content by Digging it. Popular content appears on the homepage of the Digg site and can lead to increased visibility of your content. In 2015, the company claimed that it had about 11 million active monthly members.

DM (direct messages) – a private message between social media users.

- E -

Ecommerce messenger – Ecommerce Messenger is set to allow social media users to quickly and easily complete transactions within messenger. Learn more about this in our trends for 2018 blog.

Employee advocacy – the process by which a brand uses its employees to authenticate its products. Brands may reach out to their social media savvy staff to become more involved in the promotion of the company, using their own social media accounts.

Engagement – the primary purpose of social media is for you to use it as an opportunity to actively engage with customers, potential customers, friends and family. In the simplest terms, engagement is the interaction between people and brands on social networks. For example, on Facebook, engagement includes likes, comments and shares.

- F -

Facebook Live – Live lets people, public figures and business Pages share live video with their followers and friends on Facebook. According to Facebook, Live allows you to interact with your followers and friends on another level: "Field their burning questions, hear what's on their mind and check out their live reactions to gauge how your broadcast is going."

Facebook Messenger – Facebook Messenger (sometimes abbreviated as Messenger) is an instant messaging service and software application, allowing

Facebook members to chat with friends both on mobile and the desktop website.

Facebook Spaces – in a bid to take virtual reality mainstream, Facebook introduced Facebook Spaces, an interactive virtual environment allowing people to connect with friends and build their own virtual character through their profile photos.

Filter – a photographic effect that can be applied to enhance images on social media, such as offering a vintage look, black and white, sepia, altering saturation levels, and more. Snapchat regularly updates their filter and gives brands the opportunity to sponsor filters as part of their marketing strategy.

Flickr – an image and video hosting website and web services suite. Calls itself the "best online photo management and sharing application in the world".

Follow / Follower – when you follow someone on Twitter you are essentially subscribing to their updates and tweets – you are a follower. You can also follow a company or person on LinkedIn, Instagram and Snapchat.

Friends – people you connect with on Facebook. Friends can see your Facebook profile or elements of your Facebook profile depending on what you have given them access to. On Snapchat, a friend is another user you've mutually connected with (both of you have added each other as contacts within Snapchat).

- G -

Geofilter – a filter overlay that allows people to add a location illustration specific to where they are to their photos on Snapchat.

Geotag – a tag that indicates the geographical location of a photo/video published on a social network.

Geotargeting – a tactic used by brands to deliver different content to their customers based on their geographical location. It also enables brands to create specific messaging and content for exclusively relevant audiences.

Generation Z – Generation Z (also known as iGeneration, Centennials, Post-Millennials, Homeland Generation) is the demographic cohort after Millennials. Targeting this group on social media may involve tactics including authenticity content, social responsibility and geofilters.

GIF – An acronym for Graphics Interchange Format, which refers to a file format that supports both static and animated images. Only certain social networks support gifs – check out giphy.com to find gifs to share on social media.

- H -

Handle – on Twitter, a handle is the name you choose to represent yourself. It starts with "@" e.g. Hallam's is @HallamInternet.

Hashtag – a single word or phrase preceded by the # symbol to define messages relating to a particular topic. Hashtags first emerged on Twitter but are now used on almost every other social platform too.

Header image – the large banner-like images which are found at the top of both company pages and personal accounts. A recent development by Facebook means that their 'cover photo' header image can also be replaced by a cover video – providing further dynamic advertising for brands on the platform.

Hearts – a feature of the Periscope app that measures popularity. Viewers of a stream can "heart" the broadcast an infinite amount of times, which links to the streamer's popularity ranking and stats.

- I -

Impressions – the number of times a social media post has been seen by people.

Influencer – a social media user who can reach a relevant audience (whether large or small) and create awareness about a trend, topic, company, or product. They have established credibility with their audiences, and marketers work to build relationships with them in order to reach those audiences.

Instagram Stories – Photos and videos shared on your Instagram feed that disappear after 24 hours. Launched in August 2016. Also available on Facebook.

IGTV (Instagram TV) – an application owned by Instagram that allows people to post vertical videos of up to 10 minutes. Learn how to use IGTV for your brand from our blog.

- K -

- L -

LinkedIn Talent Solutions – LinkedIn has recently invested heavily in providing easy to use products for recruiters and leveraging its connections database. One of their newest innovations is LinkedIn Talent Solutions, a platform specifically for recruitment.

List – a curated group of Twitter accounts. You can create your own lists or subscribe to lists created by others.

Live Stories – Live Stories are a curated stream of user-submitted Snaps (via Snapchat) from various locations and events. People who have their location services on at the same event location will be given the option to contribute Snaps to the Live Story. The end result is a Story told from a community perspective with lots of different viewpoints.

Live Streaming – Live broadcasting through social media. This is expected to grow in 2019, especially between social media platforms and television broadcasters. Facebook, it is expected, will announce partnerships with major broadcasters to screen exclusive content.

Lurker – a social media user that observes conversations but doesn't participate.

- M -

Mention – the act of tagging another user's handle or account name in a social media message. Mentions typically trigger a notification for that user and are a key part of what makes social media "social". When properly formatted (for example, as an @mention on Twitter), a mention also acts as a link, so your audience can click through to the user's bio or profile.

Messenger bots/chatbots – chatbots are computer programs that mimic conversation with people using artificial intelligence. A way of building more personal relationships with customers, brands will increasingly use chatbots to complete simple transactions. This is something eBbay and Shopify are already using. Read more here.

- N -

Native advertising – disguised as content, native advertising is a technique that incorporates tactics including in-feed sponsored content. Native advertising generally defines the type of advertising that shows up in the flow of editorial content.

Newsfeed – a list of news posted on a particular platform. Newsfeeds exist on your Facebook profile page, on blogs and on Twitter, for example.

Notification – a message or update sharing new social media activity. For example, if somebody likes one of your Facebook photos you will receive a notification to inform you.

- O -

.

- P -

Paid social media – businesses can pay to advertise on social media – with common types being native advertising such as Facebook Ads, LinkedIn Sponsored Content, and YouTube sponsored videos. Companies can also run standard, display-style ads on some platforms.

Permalink (permanent link) – a hyperlink to a web page that is intended to remain unchanged for years (static).

Pinned tweet – a tweet that has been pinned to the top of a Twitter profile page. Pinning a tweet is a great way to feature an important announcement or update.

Podcast – a digital audio file series created by a user and available for download on the internet.

- R -

Reach – reach signifies the number of people a brand could target using advertising. It also signifies how many people have had sight of a particular post.

Regram – re-posting somebody else's Instagram post. Best practice requires acknowledgment of the original post and the use of the hashtag #regram.

Response time – refers to the time in which a brand takes to respond to engagement from a user. This can alter the brand's overall online reputation, especially in response to queries and complaints.

Retargeting – an advertising technique in which you send content to the people who have already visited the website or page once.

Retweet – a tweet that is re-shared to the followers of another user's Twitter account. Retweeting helps to share news and build relationships with others on Twitter.

- S -

Sentiment analysis – the process of analyzing user comments or posts with the purpose of identifying the writer's attitude towards the subject – negative, neutral or positive. More about this technique on Brandwatch.

Share – the main focus of all social media platforms is to share your content, thoughts and company voice with others. Sharing options can also be added to your site, allowing people to like, +1, email or tweet you, as a method of endorsing or forwarding your content to others.

Share of voice – the number of times your brand has been mentioned in comparison with the total number of times your competitors have been mentioned online or on social media.

Shopping tags – Instagram shopping tags offer business pages the option to put information and price tags on their images.

Snap – a photo or video sent on Snapchat. You can add filters, text, emojis and drawings before sending to your recipient. Individual messages only last up to 10 seconds, then they are completely erased (although Snapchat has introduced a replay feature that allows you to have one more view).

Social mention – a social networking search engine that allows you to search the internet for social content such as blogs, comments, bookmarks, events, news, videos. Google also allows you to search blog, video and image content.

- T -

Trending – refers to a topic that is especially popular on social media at a given moment. Originating with Twitter, people add hashtags to particular words to join the discussion surrounding a topic. This can improve engagement with posts.

Troll – a word that is used to describe someone who deliberately tries to offend others on social media, often posting abusive messages to a particular individual or group to get a reaction.

Tweet – the name given to messages posted on Twitter. Tweets are microblog messages that can be a maximum of 280 characters in length.

Tone of voice – playful, educational, satirical. The tone of voice is the persona a brand portrays on social media to their audience.

- U -

User-generated content – using uploads by customers on their own social media platforms, UGC is the process in which brands repost pictures onto their main social pages. This provides an authentic endorsement, while adding volume to content already in place.

- V -

Viral marketing – a marketing technique where information is passed electronically from one internet user to another, leading to extensive coverage and high-interest levels.

Virtual reality – 360 photos launched on Facebook in June 2016, and are seen as a first step towards offering virtual reality on social media. The next logical step would be to offer 360 video content. Twitter has already announced it will be launching something similar in the new year.

Visual first – the idea that video, images and other visual content dominates social media (over text-based content).

Visual search – a feature on Pinterest that allows brands to join the dots between photos and products – improving the search function beyond hashtags towards image content.

Vlogging – the practice of regularly posting vlogs (video blogs) online.

- W -

Webinar – online seminars or presentations held by an individual or team to teach or inform about a topic to an audience. These are available pre-recorded or live streamed. However, anyone looking to take part may have to sign up to gain access.

- Y -

GLOBAL DIRECTORY OF SOCIAL MEDIA SITES

From science fiction to teens to international languages, below is a directory of social media sites covering various interests. It's incredible to see people engaging in so many different discussions and making connections around the world of planet Earth.

Social Network	Description / Focus
Academia.edu	Social networking site for academics/researchers
About.me	Social networking site
aNobii	Books
Asian Avenue	A social network for the Asian American community
aSmallWorld	European jet set and social elite worldwide
Athlinks	Running, swimming
Audimated.com	Independent music
Biip.no	Norwegian community
BlackPlanet	Black Americans

Busuu Language learning community (headquartered in Madrid, Spain)

Social Network	Description / Focus
Buzznet	Music and pop-culture
CafeMom	Mothers
Care2	Green living and social activism
CaringBridge	Not for profit providing free websites that connect family and friends during a serious health event, care and recovery.
CarSwap	Car swap and sales matching platform.
Classmates.com	School, college, work and the military
Cloob General.	Popular in Iran
Commonground	Environmental and property due diligence professionals
CouchSurfing	Worldwide network for making connections between travelers and the communities they visit.
CozyCot	East Asian and Southeast Asian women

Social Network	Description / Focus
Crunchyroll	Anime and forums.
Cucumbertown	Networking for cooks

Social Network	Description / Focus

Social Network	Description / Focus
Cyworld	General. Popular in South Korea.
DailyStrength	Medical & emotional support community - physical health, mental health, support groups
DeviantArt	Art community
Diaspora*	Decentralized, user-owned, open source, nonprofit, privacy-aware, general
Disaboom	People with disabilities (amputees, cerebral palsy, MS, and other disabilities)
Dol2day	Politic community, social network, Internet radio (German-speaking countries)
DontStayIn	Clubbing (primarily UK)
douban	Chinese Web 2.0 website providing user review and recommendation services for movies, books, and music.

Doximity	U.S. physicians and medical doctors.
Dreamwidth	Blogging.

Social Network	Description / Focus
DXY.cn	Chinese online community for physicians, health care professionals, pharmacies and facilities
Elftown	Community and wiki around fantasy and sci-fi.
Ello	Community for those who work in the creative field
Elixio	Business executives jet set and global elite.
English, baby!	Students and teachers of English as a second language
Eons.com	For baby boomers and mature internet users age 40 and beyond.
eToro	Social investing, finance
Experience Project	Life experiences

Facebook	General: photos, videos, blogs, apps.
FilmAffinity	Movies and TV series
Filmow	
FledgeWing	Entrepreneurial community targeted towards worldwide university students
Flixster	Movies
Social Network	**Description / Focus**
Flickr	Photo sharing, commenting, photography related networking, worldwide
Focus.com	Business-to-business, worldwide
Fotki	Photo sharing, video hosting, photo contests, journals, forums, flexible privacy protection, friend's feed, audio comments and unlimited custom design integration.
Foursquare	Location-based mobile social network
Friendica	Distributed, federated, privacy-aware, open source, general

Fyuse   A spatial photography app
and website which lets people capture and share
interactive 3D images.

Gab.com   Social networking service
created as an alternative to social networks like
Facebook, Twitter and Reddit.

Gaia Online   Anime and games.
Popular in United States, Canada and Europe.
Moderately popular around Asia.

GamerDNA   Computer and video
games

Social Network	Description / Focus
Gapyear.com	Travel social network
Geni.com	Families, genealogy
Gentlemint	Community for sharing

and discussing all things manly

GetGlue   Social network for
entertainment.

Gogoyoko   Fair play in music - social
networking site for musicians and music lovers.

Goodreads   Library cataloging, book
lovers.

Goodwizz   Social network with
matchmaking and personality games to find new
contacts. Global, based in France.

GovLoop   For people in and around
government.

Grono.net   Poland

HabboGeneral for teens.   Over 31 communities
worldwide. Chat room and user profiles.

hi5   General. Popular
in Nepal, Mongolia, Thailand, Romania, Jamaica, Cen
tral Africa, Portugal and Latin America. Not very
popular in the United States.

Hospitality Club   Hospitality

Social Network   **Description / Focus**

HR.com   Social networking site
for human resources professionals.

Hub Culture   Global influencers focused
on worth creation.

Ibibo   Talent-based social
networking site that allows people to promote
themselves and discover new talent. Most popular
in India.

Identi.ca   Twitter-like service popular
with hackers and software freedom advocates.

Indaba Music   Online collaboration for
musicians, remix contests, and networking.

Influenster   Online product sampling
and review platform.

Instagram   A photo and video sharing
site owned by Facebook.

IRC-Galleria   Finland

italki   Language learning social
network. 100+ languages.

Itsmy   Mobile community
worldwide, blogging, friends, personal TV-shows

Jaiku   General. Microblogging.
Owned by Google

Social Network   **Description / Focus**

Jiepang   Location-based mobile
social network. In the Chinese language

Kaixin001   General. In Simplified
Chinese; caters for mainland China residents

Kiwibox   General.

LaiBhaari   Marathi social networking

Social Network	Description / Focus
Last.fm	Music
Late Night Shots	Message boards, member profile pages, spotting other members
LibraryThing	Book lovers
Lifeknot	Shared interests, hobbies
LinkedIn	Business and professional networking
LinkExpats	Social networking website for expatriates. 100+ countries.
Listography	Lists. Autobiography
LiveJournal	Blogging. Popular in Russia and among the Russian-speaking diaspora abroad.
Livemocha	Online language learning
Makeoutclub	General

Social Network	**Description / Focus**
Mastodon	Micro-blogging
MEETin	General
Meetup (website)	General. Used to plan offline meetings for people interested in various activities

139

MillatFacebook	General, created in response to Facebook [162]

Minds	Free, open source, decentralized, and based on a foundation of transparency and privacy

mixi	Japan

MocoSpace	Mobile community, worldwide

MOG	Music

MouthShut.com	Social network, social media, consumer reviews

Mubi	Auteur cinema

MyHeritage	Family-oriented social network service

Myspace	General

Nasza-klasa.pl	School, college and friends. Popular in Poland

Nexopia	Canada

Social Network	**Description / Focus**
Ning	People create their own social websites and social networks

Odnoklassniki   Connect with old classmates. Popular in Russia and former Soviet republics

Open Diary   First online blogging community, founded in 1998

PatientsLikeMe   Online community for patients with life-changing illnesses to find other patients like them, share their data with others, and learn more about their condition to improve their outcome.

Partyflock   Dutch virtual community for people interested in house music and other electronic dance music.

Pinterest   Online pin board for organizing and sharing things you love

Plaxo   Aggregator

Playfire   Computer and video games

Playlist.com   General, music

Plurk   Micro-blogging, RSS, updates. Very popular in Taiwan

Social Network   **Description / Focus**

141

Poolwo India	Social networking site from
Quechup	General, friendship, dating
Quora	Questions and answers
Qzone	General. In Simplified Chinese; caters for mainland China residents
Raptr	Video games
Ravelry	Knitting and crochet
Reddit	A social news aggregator, social bookmarking and social discussion site. Third most-visited site in the U.S. and sixth in worldwide. [209]
Renren	Significant site in China. Was known as 校内 (Xiaonei) until August 2009.
ReverbNation.com	Social network for musician and bands
Rooster Teeth	Social network and community site
Ryze	Business
Shelfari	Books
Sina Weibo	Social microblogging site in mainland China.

Social Network	Description / Focus
Skoob	Collaborative social network for Brazilian readers
Skyrock	Social network in French-speaking world
SocialVibe	Social network for charity
Sonico.com	General. Popular in Latin America and Spanish and Portuguese speaking regions.
SoundCloud	Repository of original music pieces and networking.
Spaces	Russian social network targeted to mobile phone users
Spot.IM	A service for webmasters to add social networking functionality to their websites
Stage 32	US-based social network and educational site for creative professionals in film, television and theater
Streetlife	UK based. Links members according to where they live
StudiVZ	University students, mostly in the German-speaking countries. School students

and those out of education sign up via its partner sites schülerVZ and meinVZ.

Social Network	Description / Focus
Students Circle Network	A social network connecting students, teachers and institutions to course resources, study groups and learning spaces.
StumbleUpon	Stumble through websites that match users' selected interests
Tagged	General.
Talkbiznow	Business networking
Taringa! Argentina)	General (primarily
TeachStreet	Education / learning / teaching - more than 400 subjects
TermWiki	Learning / languages / translation - 1.2 million terms in more than 1300 subjects
The Sphere	A private online social luxury network with exclusive personalized services
TravBuddy.com	Travel
Travellerspoint	
Tsu	General

tribe.net

Tuenti   Spanish-based university
and high school social network.

Social Network	Description / Focus
Tumblr	Microblogging platform and social networking website.
Twitter	General. Micro-blogging, RSS, updates
Tylted network	Mobile social game
Uplike	General
VK	General, including music upload, listening and search. Popular in Russia and former Soviet republics.
Vampirefreaks.com	Gothic and industrial subculture
Viadeo	Global social networking and campus networking available in English, French, German, Spanish, Italian and Portuguese
Virb	Social network that focuses heavily on artists, including musicians and photographers

Wattpad   For readers and authors to interact and e-book sharing

Warm Showers   For bicycle travelers that is used to arrange free and non-obligatory homestays and hospitality

Social Network	Description / Focus
WAYN	Travel and lifestyle
WeeWorld	Teenagers - 9 to 17
We Heart It	Image-based social network focused on inspiration, expression and creativity
Wellwer	Community without borders, where sharing is everything.
Wepolls.com	Social polling network
Wer-kennt-wen	General
weRead	Books
Wooxie	Blogging and micro-blogging
WriteAPrisoner	Networking inmates, friends, family
Xanga	Blogs and "metro" areas
XING	Business (primarily Europe (Germany, Austria, Switzerland))

Xt3   Catholic social networking, created for World Youth Day 2008

Yammer   Social networking for office colleagues

Yelp, Inc.   Local business review and talk

Social Network	Description / Focus
Yookos games.	General: photos, videos, blogs,
Zoo.gr	Greek web meeting point

ABOUT THE AUTHOR

 CEO of Savvy Intrapreneur, a technology consulting and leadership development company.

CARL E. REID is a Speaker, Author, Social Media Influencer at the intersections of Technology, Leadership, Business Mentorship | Fundraising Marathon Runner | USMC Veteran

From the mail room to the board room, working at 50 companies over 50 years, Carl knows what it takes to be successful as a career employee, serial entrepreneur and business startup consultant.

Author of 2 books and several articles about networking, Carl is an expert in business relationship management. Mr. Reid has mentored many people to maneuver their careers around the uncertain job landscape and start successful freelance businesses.

Connect with Carl: CarlEReid.com | RunCARLRun.com Twitter.com/CarlEReid | LinkedIn.com/in/CarlEReid Facebook.com/CarlEReid | Instagram.com/CarlEReid

PLEASE WRITE A BOOK REVIEW AT
amazon.com/author/carlereid
Schedule a complimentary career coaching or business startup mentoring call with Carl at
Calendly.com/CarlEReid

ADDITIONAL PUBLICATIONS BY CARL E. REID

BOOKS
Visit amazon.com/author/carlereid to write a review.

10 Powerful Networking Secrets of Influential People

10 Powerful Networking Tips Using Business Cards Global Extended Edition

10 Powerful Networking Tips Using Social Media
ARTICLES

10 Powerful Networking Tips Using Evernote
Linkedin.com/pulse/10-powerful-networking-tips-using-evernote-carl-e-reid-csi-ecc

10 Powerful Linkedin Networking Tips (Part I)
Linkedin.com/pulse/10-powerful-linkedin-networking-tips-part-i-carl-e-reid-csi

10 Powerful Linkedin Networking Tips (PART II)
Linkedin.com/pulse/10-powerful-linkedin-networking-tips-part-ii-carl-e-reid-csi

VIDEO Tutorial: 12 Fearless Strategies To Pay For College and Graduate Debt Free
Linkedin.com/pulse/video-10-fearless-strategies-pay-college-graduate-carl-e-reid-csi

CAN I ASK A FAVOR?

If you enjoyed this book, found the shared information useful or of value to your career or business, I sincerely appreciate you posting a brief review on Amazon for other people to read your honest feedback.

I do read all the reviews personally so that I can continually provide actionable information in future publications that people can use to improve the quality of their life and share with their family or friends.

To leave a review for this book, please visit my Amazon Author page amazon.com/author/carlereid Then click on *10 Powerful Networking Tips Using Social Media*

Thank YOU So much for your much-appreciated support!